CAPE COD
AND THE ISLANDS
A PICTURE BOOK TO REMEMBER HER BY

Designed and Produced by
TED SMART and DAVID GIBBON

CRESCENT BOOKS
NEW YORK

INTRODUCTION

Bestowed with nature's greatest gift of beauty, Cape Code, with its miles of sandy beaches laced with cool, clear lakes and streams, lays claim to a unique part of America's past and present.

Situated in south east Massachusetts the Cape is, geologically, a mere baby, created at the end of the Ice Age just two million years ago, and given its shape of a crooked finger by a melting glacier moulding the surrounding sand.

Discovered in 1602 by an English navigator, the bay was given its name after the enormous schools of cod fish found there, but by far the most significant historical event occurred eighteen years later in 1630 when William Bradford, a pilgrim from the overcrowded Plymouth colony nearby, received a patent from the monarchy to annex the Cape. It had many attractions for the landless pilgrims, acres of salt marsh for cattle feed, streams, ponds and harbours, but on first arrival the settlers were confronted with a wilderness punctuated only by a few Indian clearings. Soon, however, their frugal natures and policy for hard work led to a well established settlement. By 1646, four towns had been formed, Sandwich, Barnstable, Yarmouth and Eastham, but the Cape Codders could not free themselves from the strict, watchful eye of the Plymouth government. The first steps towards independence were taken when a colonial became governor, but the Crown then dealt a series of blows, firstly by sending over Sir Edmond Andros to take over the settlement and later, in 1691, by consolidating the colonies into one province called Massachusetts Bay.

In the 18th and early 19th centuries, wars continually interrupted everyday life, but when the fighting ended in 1815, a period of prosperity began, with sail making, ship building and salt industries booming. The arrival of the Civil War in 1861 soon saw the end of these industries, however, and Cape Cod was flung into near poverty with farming, fishing and the newly developed cranberry industry making a living just possible. In the 1920s the slump gradually started to reverse with the arrival of the "summer people" who, realising the beauty of the Cape's surrounding land and seascapes, built homes on the south shore.

Since then, Cape Cod has grown into being one of the country's most loved holiday spots. An undeniably compelling place, its popularity has naturally caused a great deal of change to take place over the past few years, but most Cape Codders would agree that the new seems only to complement the old and none of the magnetism has been lost. Offering three hundred miles of breathtaking coastline, the Cape is a sportsman's paradise and for those who prefer to relax, the climate is excellent and the countryside dotted with historic villages.

Not far from the Cape are two islands, Martha's Vineyard and Nantucket. Settled in the early 17th century the Vineyard was first an important whaling post. Now, a favourite haunt for artists, writers and visitors, it is a retreat of beaches, moors, fishing villages and even an American Indian settlement.

Nantucket, the other major island, lies some twenty-five miles south of the Cape. Cobblestoned streets weave picturesquely around the island, edged by mansions that date back to the days when it was a wealthy sea-faring town. Aside from the many nautical attractions, Nantucket is the site of an observatory built in commemoration of Maria Mitchell, America's first woman astrologer who was born on the island.

To travel straight round the Cape would take perhaps two days, but few people would be able to resist spending more time exploring the sites. Around every corner is something to delight somebody and by the end of the journey everybody will be enchanted by Cape Cod.

The Atlantic shore of historic Marconi Beach *left* in Wellfleet. *Overleaf* the busy town and bay of Provincetown, the first landing place of the pilgrims.

A prominent commercial fishing town, boats set out from Provincetown *overleaf* early every morning, to return later with their catches of cod, flounder and haddock. The harbour *above right* was the pilgrims' first port of call after leaving England in 1620, before moving on to Plymouth in search of more fertile farmland. In commemoration of their brief stay, the Pilgrim Monument, unmistakable against the skyline *above*, was erected. A climb to the top of its tower *right*, 352 feet above the sea, reveals a magnificent view of the Cape and, on a clear day, it is possible to see Boston, to where much of the fish is transported. Not only a fishing town, the majority of the Provincetown area is included in the Province Lands section of the Cape Cod National Seashore, featuring vast stretches of beach land, edged in many places with delightful beach huts *left*, blended by the early evening sun with the blueness of the sea.

typical fishing boat *above* docks
peacefully in Provincetown harbour while
further along, cool, spacious houses line the
waterfront *overleaf*, their balconies
overlooking the water as it laps gently
under a perfect sky. Inland, a house proudly
displays the "Star-Spangled Banner" *below*,
and the white splendour of the Town Hall
left, sits in front of a bas-relief of the signing
of the Mayflower Compact, flanked by
memorial tablets. Beautiful reconstructions
of the days when Provincetown was a
thriving whaling post, such as a captain's
quarters *right*, are displayed in the local
museum.

A seemingly unending stretch of golden beaches with some of the most spectacular sand dunes along the Atlantic coast, Provincelands *right, left and above right* was established as part of the National Seashore in 1961. Dotted with numerous exciting nooks and crannies, bicycle trails meander through more than 4,000 acres of land finely preserved in its natural state; past the beaches of Herring Cove *above and below* and Race Point *overleaf,* through ponds and leafy forests.

The elegant coastline *above and below* curves away from Provincetown to foot the Cape's least populated area of Truro, with houses discreetly tucked away in coves, along with reminders of its fluctuating historical importance. Highland Light *above left and right,* the Cape's oldest lighthouse, was built in 1797 on a stretch of land known as the "graveyard of ships". The exquisite Corn Hill Beach *overleaf* and Head of Meadow Beach *below left* are just two of the sites that grace the coastline.

Nestling in their pastoral surroundings, Ba
Village in north Truro *above,* the first
Congregational Church *above left,* and a
house near Cornhill *right,* display the
familiar Cape technique of blending
buildings with the countryside. A varied
population of sea birds visit Head of
Meadow Beach *below* and later in the day
the sun sinks slowly over Pond Village
below left, bathing its beach *overleaf* in a
pool of golden light.

A trip around the town of Wellfleet on the lower Cape would undoubtedly include a visit to Marconi Beach *these pages and overleaf* and the site of the famed Italian physicist, Guglielmo Marconi's first trans-Atlantic wireless station. Miscalculating the Wellfleet airwaves, his first circle of twenty wooden towers collapsed in 1902, but a year later, after rapid reconstruction, communication was established.

A patent received from the Earl of Warwick in 1630 annexed a large portion of land, originally called "Nawsett" to the nearby Plymouth Colony, an area which included the town of Eastham. The windmill *below* dates back to this time, but Penniman House *right* was built more than 200 years later, in 1876, by a whaling captain. Less than forty years later a Coast Guard Station was built but, due to rapidly eroding sands, was replaced in 1936. Now, the Coast Guard Beach Centre *below left*, on Coast Guard Beach *above*, serves as an environmental and educational centre. The Nauset Lighthouse *above left*, overlooks the impressive cliffs and shore of Nauset Light Beach *overleaf*.

very Cape town has its beautiful beaches
nd Eastham is no exception, with Coast
Guard Beach *right* and Nauset Light Beach
verleaf, whilst a fresh water pond on
Nauset Beach *above,* is also a familiar sight.
The surrounding countryside is laced with
xciting trails, the most famous of which,
he Forthill swamp trail *left,* passes
rchards, stone fences, old salt works and
omesites, all reminders of the historical
vents that took place in the offshore
aters. The plaque *below* commemorates
he Nauset Coast Guard Station,
sponsible for the safe anchorage of many
wayward vessel.

Long stretches of silver and golden sand folding away from the land into the sparkling sea make Eastham's coastline one of the loveliest expanses of ocean beach to be found in the country *these pages*, and features excellent facilities for sun-bathing, swimming, picnicking and much more, all under a perfect blue sky.

The elegant building *left* is Brewster's Town Hall, built in 1880, which is set in leafy grounds as serene as the waterfront *above* near Orleans. Stony Brook Mill *right,* used for grinding corn and preparing wool, still functions. The clear pond *below,* framed by burnished forest land, is part of the 2,000 acres of state park, established in memory of Roland C. Nickerson.

The distinctive "Church of the New Jerusalem" in Yarmouth *left* is the work of an Italian architect and provides a decorative contrast to the first Congregational Church in Yarmouth Port *below* and the spacious colonial Winslow Crocker House *right*. The Bass River estuary is pictured *above*.

Barnstable extends from the Bay on the north to the Sound on the south, representing all that is old and new in the Cape, from the commercial bustle of Hyannis Harbour *above* and port *below left,* to Maraspin Creek *right,* as well as Hyannis Lighthouse *top left,* charmingly enclosed by a low circle of rocks, and the colonial Courthouse *below.* A memorial to John F. Kennedy *centre left,* whose family home was in nearby Hyannisport, is a mark of respect to the esteemed President.

Barnstable Harbour *above right,* one of the most picturesque fishing marinas in the Cape, is as vivid a blue as the rolling dunes of Sandy Neck Beach *right,* are gold. From the top of Sunset Hill a view overlooking the exciting Fiddler's Green golf course *above,* extends to incorporate the Kennedy family summer home *left.* In one of the town's quiet parks lies the monument to the prominent political activist, James Otis *below.*

Mill Creek Marsh *overleaf* is set in the little village of Sandwich.

The monument *below* stands in honour of the pilgrims who sailed into Plymouth aboard the Mayflower *above*, first setting foot on the memorialised rock *left*. Dexter Grist Mill *right* and Hoxie House *above right* are in the historic town of Sandwich.
  Overleaf: Menemsha Harbour, Martha Vineyard.

An important fishing area, nets hanging out to dry *right* are a typical waterfront scene on the lovely island retreat of Martha's Vineyard in Duke's County, as is the fishing vessel *centre left*, tied up at Dutcher Docks in the quaint harbour of Menemsha *above* in Chilmark. Edgartown, with its lighthouse *below*, is connected by the little "On-Time" ferry *bottom left* to Chappaquidick, where Dyke Bridge *top left* is also sited.

Soft, pastel-coloured countryside is the perfect setting for the horse breeding farm in West Tisbury *above*. The Federated Church *above left* dates back to 1828, while the boat-shed *below left* is part of an old house, built in 1765, which belonged to Thomas Cooke, a customs collector. Oak Bluffs *below and right*, originally called Cottage City, is a village of ornately trimmed "gingerbread" cottages that line charming, narrow streets.

The Vineyard's rugged coastline *right* sweeps round to the awesome cliffs *below, and above and below left* on the majestic western headland. With their beautiful, variegated colours they are a storehouse of information for geologists. Perched high on the cliff, the lighthouse *above* erected in 1952, has guided many ships safely into Vineyard Sound.

Nantucket, the other major island, is delightfully dotted with historic villages and houses. A view inside the William Hadwen House *this page* shows off the tasteful splendour created by the Victorian colonials. The marble mantles on the fireplaces downstairs were carved from a ballast brought from Europe, whilst silver, china and glassware decorate the table tops and walls. The Keeping Room *below left* belongs to the simpler, but no less impressive, "1800 House" which served as the home for the High Sheriff of Nantucket County in the early part of the 19th century. Equally elegant, the kitchen in Jethro Coffin House *above left*, displays all the utensils common to the Victorian kitchen, a room rarely visited by the master of the house.

Nantucket's excellent harbour is always a colourful scene *left* with sleek schooners, ketches, yawls and motor boats at their moorings. Along an ancient thoroughfare called Broadway, lies the island's largest group of old dwellings including Auld Lang Syne *right* built prior to 1700, some fifty years before Job Macey House *above*. Lighthouses such as Sankaty Head *above right* overlook the surrounding waters from all directions, and Brant Point *below* guards the entrance to the harbour.

Still able to grind corn, the Old Mill *overleaf*, is the sole survivor of four mills that once stood along the range of hills west of Nantucket.

First published in 1981 by Colour Library International Ltd.
Illustrations and text © : Colour Library International Ltd, 163 East 64th Street, New York 10021.
Colour separations by FERCROM, Barcelona, Spain.
Display and text filmsetting by Focus Photoset, London, England.
Printed by Cayfosa and bound by Eurobinder - Barcelona (Spain)
Published by Crescent Books, a division of Crown Publishers Inc.
Library of Congress Catalogue Card No. 81 65046
CRESCENT 1981